# A MUSEUM of Early American TOOLS

by

## ERIC · SLOANE

BALLANTINE BOOKS · NEW YORK

Library of Congress Catalog Card Number:
64-13741

ISBN 0-345-32611-3

This edition published by arrangement with
Funk & Wagnalls, Inc.

Manufactured in the United States of America

First Ballantine Books Edition: October 1973

15  14  13  12  11  10

This sketchbook is dedicated to the
unrecorded pioneer Americans who
fashioned their own tools. Although
mass production has made their old
tools obsolete, along with Early American
individualism, these ancient implements
are symbols of a sincerity, an integrity,
and an excellency that the craftsman
of today might do well to emulate.

# A Special Tool

hollowing Gouge

Hay Fork

paring Adze

Draw-Knife

cornering a Chisel

a Fitting Mallet

Apple butter Paddle

mortising Chisel and mortising Axe

a boring Auger

a Brace

Awl

Hewing Broad Axe

a paring Stick

a Holding Dog

a pounding Commander

hauling Sledge

for every Job.

a Winnowing Tray

Raft Auger

Fencing Axe

a Splitting Froe

Reaping Hooks

Hitting Beetle

Striking Maul

a Splitting Wedge

a Hewing Hatchet

CHISEL BIT

KNIFE BIT

a Felling Axe

a Barking Spud

Trading Axes

Propping Saw horse

The Carpenter who
builds a good House to
defend us from Wind and
Weather, is far more
serviceable than the
curious Carver who
employs his art to
please his Fancy...

...from an old tool pamphlet...
..1719

# Author's Note

I like the sound of the word museum. Perhaps because the word root refers less to an actual collection of things than to the musing, cogitating, and reflecting that one does while beholding a collection.

Nowadays we use the word museum to identify a big, housed collection, but in the days of Early America it usually meant a simple library or some printed collection of facts. There were magazinelike books, such as "Merry's *Museum*," and there were newspaperlike publications, such as "The Farmer's *Museum*," but the fine word museum has since drifted from the world of writing. Because it is my hobby to recapture what I believe to be the good things of the past, I hope the reader will accept and enjoy my title, *A Museum of Early American Tools*.

The word magazine was first used to identify what we now might call a museum; it then meant "storehouse," or "housed collection" (powder magazine, for instance). And the first printed magazines were (like the newspapers of that day) printed on one piece of paper and folded once or perhaps twice—never in the book-form of today's magazine.

In presenting my collection of drawings as a museum, I hope that it will, like a scrapbook, induce musing and reflecting, and that it will draw the reader back into the quite different world of Early America. The rambling sequence of subjects is no accident: I would like my reader to "stroll" through this book as he would through a museum.

We might regard some of the old tools as clumsy or ugly unless we look at them in terms of the century in which they were used. Many of today's tools would have been considered ugly, clumsy, and completely undesirable by the early craftsmen. The steel and plastic handles we now

*xi*

have, for example, lack the spring and "feel" of seasoned wood that experts know. Shovels were made of wood not because of a lack of metal (as many assume) but because it was supposed that grain and apples were harmed by contact with metal. You might think of a wooden shovel as being short-lived, yet, although thousands of wooden shovels are to be found in antique shops and collections, almost no early metal shovels remain.

Most of today's tools have the cheapness of mass production; the old hand-made tools often had design that made them examples of fine art. Lumber cut and sold as a "two by four" was once an honest two inches by four inches; even today there are people who are shocked to learn that our lumber, because it is measured before being trimmed and planed, is sold at a quite untrue measurement. Builders who constructed rooms that were not accurately square (and why should they be?) are now regarded as slipshod and careless; yet the old buildings have stood the test much better than will many we are now building, for the joints and braces were made with much greater care than today's craftsmen consider "necessary." Floor boards were never the same width at one end as they were at the other. Quaint or poor workmanship? Not at all. The finished effect is finer than the monotony of today's narrow-width floor boards. A building pinned together with hand-whittled wooden pins? We don't have to do that sort of thing today! But if we built for lastingness and for handing down to future generations we would do so, for wooden pins work much better than nails: they hold tighter, they don't rust and rot the beams.

While I was putting this book together, my neighbor bought a good new saw and left it out overnight in the dew. Its shiny newness had given way to the orange of rust, and he telephoned me to ask for help in removing it. I took it to clean and loaned him one of my early saws to use in the meantime. The old saw was one I found in the stone wall of an ancient barn. It is still sharp and clean of rust.

And so it goes. The craftsman of yesterday might look like a poorly informed man only before we take a longer and a better look. His tools might appear pathetically poor, but his ways were honest and lasting and beautiful to an extent that is today deemed over and above requirements. How poor and dishonest and ugly and temporary are the results of so many modern workers whose constant aim is more to make the most money from their profession instead of producing the most honest and beautiful and lasting things. I feel that a good way of studying the conscience and personality of the anonymous pioneer American—so that I may emulate some of his ways—is by collecting and analyzing the tools with which he worked.

*As a collector of early tools, I have also been a collector of information. Antique implements have a price tag on them, but for the information that has been priceless and gratis, I am indebted to the men at Doylestown, Shelburne, Winterthur, Cooperstown, Sturbridge, Williamsburg, and Saugus. I learned much from two excellent books, Mercer's* Ancient Carpenters' Tools *and Wildung's* Woodworking Tools, *and from the Early American Industries Association's publication,* The Chronicle.

Eric Sloane

Weather Hill

*The lines of the early tools were traditional, functional, honest, beautiful in a harmonious simplicity.*

# Contents

# a Museum of Early American Tools

# The Romance of Tools.

Finding an ancient tool in a stone fence or in a dark corner of some decaying barn is receiving a symbol from another world, for it gives you a particular and interesting contact with the past. Men used to build and create as much for future generations as for their own needs, so their tools have a special message for us and our time. When you hold an early implement, when you close your hand over the worn wooden handle, you know exactly how it felt to the craftsman whose hand had smoothed it to its rich patina. In that instant you are as close to that craftsman as you can be—even closer than if you live in the house that he built or sit in the chair that he made. In that moment you are near to another being in another life, and you are that much richer.

Why an ancient tool should be closer to the early craftsman than a modern tool is to a modern workman is not readily understood by most people. Even the ardent collector is sometimes unaware of the reason an ancient tool meant so much to its user. But reason there is. Henry Ward Beecher said it nicely when he explained that "a tool is but the extension of a man's hand." Whereas today's implements are designed with the idea of "getting a job done quickly," there was an added quality to the early implements and an added quality to early workmanship too. For, like the nails on a beast's paws, the old tools were so much an extension of a man's hand or an added appendage to his arm, that the resulting workmanship seemed to flow directly from the body of the maker and to carry something of himself into the work. True, by looking at an old house or an old piece of furniture, you can imagine the maker much more clearly than you can by beholding anything made today.

The early implement was also a piece of art, as much as the work it

2

## Like extensions of the Human Hand.

fashioned, for the worker designed his tools too. In Early America the ironworkers forged only the cutting blade; they gave no thought to the design of the wooden handle and the rest of the finished tool. Plane blades and even knife-blades were hand-forged and sold like axe heads, and the craftsman was left to make his own wooden "hand" to hold the "fingernail," or cutting part. A small hand needed a small handle and a big hand needed a big handle; the man who used an apprentice had notches in his big plane that enabled the apprentice to help push it along with a stick.

A man whose architectural creations followed the Greek or Roman tradition would find it natural to include Greek or Roman artistic touches in the ornamentation of his implements. Decoration on the early tool, however, sprang from the pride of the maker rather than from any custom.

The feeling that certain tools had souls of their own was not unusual; an axe might be marked "Tom" or "Jack" simply because the owner felt it was a companion worthy of a pet name. All this sounds strangely superstitious. Yet today motor trucks are often named "Sally" or "Babe"; boats almost always have names; even large machine tools, such as presses or bulldozers, are graced with pet names.

*Sacred initials on one side, the date on the other.*

The religious man probably felt that sacred initials or Biblical quotations might have their effect upon the work done by that tool. Perhaps mindful that the carpenter Jesus once worked with such tools, some of the early woodworking implements have crosses carved upon them.

One of the finer pieces in a recent showing of modern art was a piece of steel that curved like a bird's wing. It was set into a square block of wood and its title in the catalogue was "Number 1760." The artist had an even more honest sense of beauty than a sense of humor, for if you looked closely and with an informed eye, you could recognize the piece as the head of an Early American "goose wing" broad axe. In the back of the blade, the year 1760 had been marked, which, of course, explained the title. To many it was, at first, the most beautiful piece of art there,

*Germanic Northern Pennsylvania*

but when they learned that it was only an old axe head, they felt as if they had been hoaxed. How, after all, could an axe head be considered a work of art!

The Civil War period marked a turning point in tool design, as it did for so much Americana. Before that time, the word tool meant an implement that could make one thing at a time; mass-production tools then entered the scene, and the word tool, which had meant only "hand tool," took on many added meanings. Finally the word tool came to mean any item having to do with the production of an item; it could be the machine and also the building that housed the machine. Even the salesmen, the advertising gadgets, and the business offices are "tools of the trade."

Generally speaking, hand tools made after the Civil War period lacked the simple beauty of those of the ante-bellum period. Things were made to sell quickly, things were made in large quantities so that they could be catalogued identically, and hand-made implements began to disappear. Wooden handles became "fancier," more curved and ornamental, but the severe beauty of folk art and primitive usage was lost. Saw handles became "trickier"; they were designed to appeal to the eye instead of to fit the hand. Axe handles, which had always been almost straight, as a good club should be, took on curves such as the "fawn foot" and the "scroll knob." By 1885, handles on axes and adzes had become almost too curved, but by the 1900's they settled down to a sensible and standard design, such as that of those you can buy now at the hardware store.

Before the Civil War, most axe handles (like the handles of all tools) were made by the man who would use the axe. A pattern was cut from a piece of flat wood and saved as the model from which future handles would be fashioned. Axe patterns (which you can still find in old barns) were so subtly curved and proportioned that they were as distinctive as a man's signature; you could take one look and say "This tool belongs to Jones" or "That tool belongs to Smith." Very often an axe-handle pattern was handed down from generation to generation, and it was considered counterfeit for another family to copy it.

While we are on the subject of the handles of old tools, I would like to point out that the collector should understand something of the philosophy about the connection between the workman's hand and that

5

part of a hand tool that he touches. Most modern workmen will scoff at the idea, but any fine craftsman will tell you that the right wooden handle (let us say, on a hammer) helps you along with your work. A metal or plastic handle or even an incorrect wooden handle can feel "dead" and not "spring back" against pressure, thus causing blisters and slowing your work. The proper handle's "feel" or "heft" is the unexplainable quality that a fine violin has to the musician. *The Oxford History of Technology* quotes Christian Barman's comments on an exhibition of early hand tools: "Everybody who appreciates the qualities of materials loves wood, and here was wood formed into a special kind of tactile sculpture made to be felt with the hand. I remembered that old craftsmen, when they buy a new set of modern chisels, throw away the handles and carefully fit their own. These handles, polished bright by a lifetime of use, became part of their owners' lives."

Always in the fine art of working with wood, the old-time craftsman's laboratory was in his head and his hands and his heart. He called it "knack"; some now believe it was a "sixth sense" or an extrasensory power. Elusive as this "knack" may be, it is the most important part of those small differences that distinguish the master craftsman from the good workman.

When we consider tools, we are dealing with human benefactors of the most primary sort. Tools increase and vary human power; they economize human time, and they convert raw substances into valuable and useful products. So when we muse on historic tools as symbols, we are always analyzing the romance of human progress.

Although Early American tools were traditional in design to such an extent that one can usually tell the nationality of the maker, there are almost always subtle differences and decorative touches in design that equally identify the region of American countryside from which the tool came. A collector can easily tell a piece coming from Pennsylvania from one originating in Connecticut. This distinctiveness was often intentional; the Early American's urge for identification was born of pride both in himself and in his time. An extraordinary awareness of life and time permeated our early days; when something was made and the maker was satisfied, it wasn't complete until his mark and the date were added.

Nowadays things are almost obsolete before they leave the drawing board. How lucky we are that so many of the old tools and the things that were made with them were dated and touched with the craftsman's art.

pre-Civil War

by 1885

"Fawn Foot"

"Scroll Knob"

"Swell Knob"

—an axe-handle pattern was part of every man's tool kit.

# Crude Shops, Magnificent Results.

After the Civil War, factory-made things became popular and the tool house was limited to such minor work as farm repairs. The Dominy Shop (shown below) was used by Nathaniel Dominy IV (1737–1812) and his son Nathaniel V (1770–1852). This entire shop, including manuscript accounts covering the period from 1762 until 1829, has been kept intact at the Henry Francis du Pont Winterthur Museum in Delaware. The visitor's first reaction is usually "What a primitive shop!" Yet the magnificent table standing in the center of the room was made in it.

*Courtesy, Henry Francis du Pont Winterthur Museum*

Tool House in Berks County Pennsylvania

PLANK TO BE SAWED AT X
IS HELD AND LIFTED BY
Side Rest

BENCH HOOK Ⓐ

an old-time
Carpenter-bench

HOLES FOR BENCH HOOKS

HOLES FOR A Hold-fast
FOR CLAMPING DOWN BOARDS.

Horizontal Bench vise

Vertical vise

Ⓐ

Ⓑ

Bench Clamp

Block Knife

Block Hook

PIECE OF WOOD
HELD BY STOP Ⓐ Ⓑ
IN A
Box Vise

9

# An Ax is an Axe!

No matter how you spell it (both ways are correct), it is natural to start off a sketchbook of Early American implements with this tool. America was a new world of unending wood where a man armed with only a felling axe could enter the forest and survive. With his axe he could clear the land of trees, cut fuel, build a bridge, a house, and furniture. With his axe he could fashion snares for game and, in a pinch, use it to protect himself against marauding Indians or wild beasts. No wonder the first settlers carried axes in their belts and treated them with a respect like that of a soldier toward his sword or side arms.

As was true of all first American artifacts, our earliest axes were like those from abroad. They had well-curved, gracefully fashioned blades, and they lacked the bulky polls such as those that identify the pure American design. The heavy poll appears to be for hammering (indeed it could have been used for such), yet it was devised to serve as a weight to give more momentum to chopping. Few early polless axes have survived except those traded with the Indians (trade axes).

These TRADE AXES were made for trading with
the Indians...

1730

...no wonder tomahawks were
designed after them!

Nearly Square, the American-made Pre-Revolutionary Axe had a poll or head (A) outweighing its bit (B)

A

B

1740

...another American Axe

early Western triangular

about 1790

POLL

Here were the Earliest designs

no poll

First hint of poll

about 1715

1600's

German

British

Anglo-American

# A World of Axes

America's wealth of wood and her pride in carpenter craftsmanship resulted in an amazing array of specialty tools. Early catalogues listed more than fifty patterns of axe heads alone, all doing the same jobs yet differing in design. Farmers and blacksmiths fashioned their own axes for framing and for mortising the beams of barns (shown below) or for felling trees (shown opposite).

*about 1760* — **Mortise Axes** *were like chisels, pounded on their heads —*

*1820*

*to make square holes for tenons*

*pounding surfaces*

*a rare 2-bladed Mortise Axe*

**Chisel Axe.** *Pennsylvania (1700's) ...had a small wood handle.(x)*

*MORTISE HOLE*

*Axes* were made by folding an iron pattern, adding a steel wedge.

1.

2.

HANDLE PATTERN

3. then the axe was hammered over a metal handle pattern until shaped.

hammer welded

-- this process was used till the end of the 1800's.

*British type* (Maine 1750)

*German type* (Penn. 1740)

*Kent type* about 1780

*Ship·builder's* about 1800 (New Hampshire.)

*Joiner's Axes*

(R.I.) about 1760

# The Broad Axe

A most essential Early American tool was the chisel-edged broad axe. Thousands of them are still around, but people seeing this broad axe often take it for a very big and clumsy felling axe. Because few museums bother either to include the tool or to explain its use, few people really know how it was used. Actually, it was a kind of plane or striking chisel that early Americans used for hewing round logs into square beams.

More than twice the size of a felling axe, this tool had a short bent handle protruding outward from the side of the axe head with the bevel (basil or chisel-slant) on that same side. Two hands were used; the process was called "squaring" or "hewing."

The American-style broad axe had a fair-sized squarish head, or poll (as the other American-style axes did); European types had none.

Although hand-hewn timbers in old buildings are commonly called "adzed beams," they were usually broad-axed.

Although some odd people hack up beams "to make them appear hand done," the most expert broad-axe man cut the fewest axe marks, and those that were left were spaced nicely—never haphazardly.

*Never haphazard!*

Exaggerated here, you see the flat side of the axe against the log; chisel or basilled side out. (NOTICE HANDLE ALSO BENDS OUT.)

Chisel or basilled side.

Seen from above, handles were bent away from the log. x (to protect fingers.)

BENT    x

SWAYED    x

FELLING AXE

BROAD AXE

KNIFE EDGE is for Felling.

CHISEL EDGE is for Hewing.

Three Major Broad Axe Types.

POLL

ENGLISH

GERMAN

American Broad Axe    Polless Broad Axe    Goose wing

L.I. N.Y. about 1640

Much of early hewing has yet to be explained . . .

. . . the ancient European Broad Axe was a strange tool.

DUG UP AT JAMESTOWN

15

# How the Broad Axe was Used.

Any old-timer is willing to tell you how to use a broad axe, but each one is bound to describe a different method. Trying to ferret out the truth I asked everyone who visited my collection—if the visitor claimed he knew the art—to demonstrate broad-axing. Some "used to stand upon the log, hewing as they walked along it." "But you wouldn't be able to reach the log with so short a handle! You'd chop your toes off!" was my reply. But they insisted, and offered to demonstrate. The doctor managed to sew one toe back on very nicely.

Actually, a walk-along-the-log method was used, but with a special broad axe unlike the ancient ones with bent handles. (This is shown on the following page.) As for the ancient chisel-edged broad axe, you walked *alongside* the log, working as you went. One man would swing horizontally (with the grain); another would hit straight downward; another would strike at an angle. As for me, I contend there was no generally accepted procedure. Mercer (in *Ancient Carpenters' Tools*) says that the broad axe was usually "held with both hands, right hand foremost. The leg face was set against the workman's left side and he hewed with both hands, not longways with the grain but diagonally *downward* across it."

"DOGS" were used to fasten logs to be worked upon.

two types

*Broad-axing* began with a *Chalk-Line* as the
log was bark-stripped
to the brown under-bark
and "twanged" with a
*Squaring Cord.*

MAKING CHALK-LINE AT A

CHALK

① X                                    X

X                                                            X

② *First standing on the log*
with a long-handled
*Felling Axe*

"Scoring to the Line"

and scoring
deep vertical
cuts.

Dog

Often the pieces between
intervals
          were split off.

③

...then standing *alongside.*

"Hewing to the Line."

*Holding* the *Broad axe*
with two hands, right
hand foremost          and
left knee close to the log,
the final smooth-hewing was done

17

# A Giant and a Midget:

The straight-handled broad axe—a knife-edged axe beveled on both sides—was usually used to hew railroad ties. Logging railroads that make their ties out of softwood hew just two sides of the log. A tree was felled at a slight angle (held at one end by its own branches), and the hewer walked first up and then down, flattening the sides as he went. The same axe was used both for scoring and hewing! This process seems difficult but it was fast.

Because this axe has a straight handle, it is often mistaken for some re-handled ancient broad axe, ground on two sides to convert it into a felling axe. The only clue to its true use is that its ponderous head is much too heavy to swing sideways as an axe must be swung in felling.

The smallest version of the hewing axe is the carpenter's hewing hatchet (below). It sometimes looks like a toy model of the big one. Never used to split wood or to drive nails, these hatchets were used for shaping.

a tiny Carpenter's Hewing Hatchet

about 1725

3¼"

side view.

*a more recent Broad Axe.*

1895

3 ft.

Sharpened on *both* sides

1.

2.

up

down

Ties. .
8 feet long

*Cutting railroad ties*

The Hewing Hatchet    (before 1820)

about 1 ft.

often with
Straight
handles

1800

Eye is
bulged
on *one* side.

1750

*One* side is
Sharpened.

Carpenter's
Shaper

# The Hatchet.

Today's household hatchet began as the "shingling hatchet." This had a flared shape with slightly rounded nail-hammering head and a nail-pulling notch in the bit. Because the first New World roofs were thatched, shingling hatchets were unknown to the early settler. Shingling hatchets so often fell from roofs being worked on that roofers frequently had them strung for hanging at the wrist.

The "lathing hatchet" is recognized by its flat outside contour, made so nails could be struck near a ceiling without hitting it. If the axe head flared, the flare was on the inside of the bit. It soon became the favorite carpenter's tool to replace the awkward cooper's hatchet. (See opposite. The cooper rounding off a barrel head is using a cooper's hatchet; notice how it was held close to its head rather than by the end of its handle.)

The 1790 American axe-hatchet (shown below) was a miniature model of the square-headed American axe with the poll that outweighed the bit.

a 1790 *Hatchet* (axette)

the First American design

the Earliest Factory-made *Hatchets*

(about 1845)

The *Shingling Hatchet* had a long nail-hammering poll → and flared bit.

Original handle often had hole or eye for a string.

(x)

Maine        N.J.

Ceiling surface was cleared by the flat end (x) of the

*Lathing Hatchet*

LATH

6"

1780

*Cooper's Hatchet* for shaping

# Hammers

The claw hammer hasn't changed much since about 75 A.D. Aside from its aesthetic qualities, the Roman example shown below has a most efficient design (which might do well to show up any day now).

The use of nails in the 1600's and the 1700's was more efficient then than now. The early square-cut nails, for instance, had greater holding power than our round nails; furthermore, they retarded splitting of the wood. The practice of "clinching" (bending over the protruding point) is now regarded as poor workmanship, but its efficiency is obvious. Early batten doors with wrought nails on the outside and bent points on the inside are cemented together so well that it is next to impossible to pry them apart.

Perhaps the rarity of ancient iron hammers in America is due to the once widespread practice of using wooden mallets to drive in wooden nails (tree-nails or trunnels), even wooden nails of a tiny toothpick size. Wooden mallets were also used as striking chisels; iron hammers, *only* for metal nails.

x

a *Roman Claw Hammer*
with contour following the motion (x)
of the tool
in use.

a *Gem of Good Designing.*

← DELICATELY ROUNDED FACE

1780

Pennsylvania *Hammers*
(not unlike
the ancient Roman.)

1761

CLAW FOR
WOODEN PEGS

early 1800's

*Cooper's Hammer*

FOR
CORNERS
OF DRAWERS

used as much
for cabinets,
was the "*Cobbler's Hammer*"

*Early nail Hammer*

(FLEXIBLE)

*Veneer Hammer*
1835

*Cooper's bungstart*

*Carpenter's Mallet*
1750

1790

hickory

*Walnut Burl Mallet*
1760

*Beech-Burl Wheelwright's Mallet*

23

# The Axe and the Log House.

Before we leave the subject of axes, the reader will be interested in seeing just what was expected of the axe. Here are some standard log-house notches often made with only the axe.

Maul and ... Mortise axe. and Saw.

Chamfer and notch

square ends

1760

Square·notch

late 1700's

...often chinked with narrow clapboards

# Saddle·notch

1. Axe cut    2. Gutter Adze to round out

# Sharp·notch ·could be done with axe alone.

← 2 slashes and
← notch below 3

1  2
3

# Dovetail·notch    came from Sweden (c.1640)

Lip adze and axe.

upper notch slants out to drain rain.

# The Adze

The idea of a sharp tool with its blade at a right angle to the handle is most ancient. The Early American version was swung in the curvature of the blade, with the arm and tool forming the radius.

Because of its flaring square end, the adze head had to be removable (as the bevel to be sharpened was on the inside and inaccessible to a grindstone). Some of the earliest adzes, however, had nonremovable heads, which had to be sharpened with a whetstone.

The shipwright's adze had a long peg-poll for driving down broken nails (and to prevent the blade from being nicked).

As shown below, the right-angle cuts on old beams are make-ready scorings for broad-axe work, not so-called "adze marks." Only on special "parlor beams" (these were made to be exposed) was the adze introduced; then the surface effect was from a delicate ripple to almost complete smoothness.

The Adze made surfaces smooth

Broad-axed beam with make ready axe scorings left showing.

- - - it didn't leave score marks.

*The adze helve (handle) has a flaring end.*
*(usually rectangular)*

*The curve came in during 1800's*

## Carpenter's Adze

FLAT POUNDING POLL

OCTAGONAL POLL

*1800's*

POLLESS

MAUL HEAD
POLL

*1600's*

NOTICE
BEVELS
ARE ON
INSIDE

*1700's*

## Shipwright's Adze *or "American adze."*

*..had a spur or nail punch.*

no poll

## The Gutter Adze.
*or "spout adze"*

*came "lipped" and "round"*

*the smaller version of this
is the one-hand*

## Cooper's Adze

*shown on next pages*

# Canoes and Bowls

The word canoe (canow and canoo in the 1600's) described a hollowed-out log. Until the Indians saw the English hand adze, they used fire to burn out the hollow portion and flint knives and shells to scrape out the burned wood. Then they devised their own adze, using flint instead of metal for the blade. The scoop, or scorp, became refined as the years went by, and, finally, it became a finishing tool.

Maple and ash burls (wartlike bumps on tree trunks) were first burned and then scorped out, making the toughest and most durable of all bowls.

The Burl (boil + knurl)
made the best bowl

a canoe trough and

an Indian "canow."

Indian adze
hide
flint
circa 1600

wedge
iron strap
1720
1720 Connecticut Hand Adze
basilled

1790
Cooper's Adze 1790
"colt's foot"
5 to 11" long

an open Scorper 1820

a rare Scorp
1800's
Side view
blade
x
x

closed Scorp

Iron scorps
1850
(straight and curved)

# Wedges and Froes

A good woodsman would never consider using his axe as a hammer to hit the head of a wedge. That would not only widen the eye but also would finally split the cheeks, finishing off the axe head forever. Yet many paintings of Lincoln show him splitting rails with an axe. Rails were split with wedges. Iron wedges (or wooden gluts) were driven into the wood with a heavy maul or beetle (as shown below).

To split shingles, laths, staves, and clapboards, a knife-type wedge called a froe or frow (shown on the opposite page) was struck with a short maul known as a froe-club. In England the froe is known also as a fromard or rending-axe. The clapboard-maker struck away from himself and twisted the froe handle to split the board with the grain, while striking away with the froe-club (see drawing).

The froe became obsolete about a century ago, when it became customary to saw-cut shingles and laths. Till then, "riving" shingles was a favorite rainy-day woodshed job, and every household had several froes on hand.

*(X ·· IRON HOOPS)*

*Rails were split by*

*Oak wedges or "Gluts"...*

*... struck with*

*a Beetle*

*or a Burl Maul*

*←— about 3½' long —→*

# The Froe

could split a block of wood

into shingles

13"

or barrel staves

a rare type of curved froe

cooper's curved froe

or clapboards

by twisting the handle as the froe is struck

# The Fine Art of Splitting

The uses of the froe were many. Very old men, too feeble to swing an axe, were given the chore of splitting kindling from logs. Half-round barrel hoops were also split with the froe. Willow poles were split in half for making gates and hurdles. The early hurdle was not like our horse hurdle; it was a section of fence that could be lashed to other similar sections to make a portable animal enclosure.

Lathing was split with the froe from fresh oak, in both single strips and "flats." Lath flats were split first on one side, then the other, making a sort of accordion piece that could be unfolded.

The saw was almost never used for cutting with the grain or lengthwise: splitting a length of wood was so much easier. A craftsman could split inch-square lengths from a large piece of wood in a fraction of the time that it would take him to saw them.

Because of the many uses of the froe, there is hardly an old barn left that doesn't have a number of these tools tucked away somewhere in it. Less ubiquitous, however, are their battered mates, the froe-clubs.

the Froe-Club
new
used

No need for a saw! Want a 1" by 2" or a 2" by 3"?

Just split a pole, twist the froe and with three more rives youve got it!

Early "accordion lath" was made by splitting an oak slab and pulling it apart.

a rare froe is the Knife Froe

—14"—

All wrought metal ... New Hampshire about 1740

# Tools with Legs

Chairmaking was one of the earliest industries of the Shakers, so it is natural that they were also pioneers in installing their wonderful mechanical appliances onto benches so that operators could sit while working. The first American shingle bench may have been made in Maine or Pennsylvania, but it reached its peak in design with the Shakers.

One Lebanon (New York) shinglemaker filled a request for 5,000 shingles in December of 1789, which, apparently, was a usual sort of output for one operator. Shaker-made broom-vices, apple parers, nailbenches, and herb-cutters were installed on legs and attached to stools of one kind or another or designed so that the buyer could affix the appliance to a bench he made himself. To sit at work was, all of a sudden, a new American pleasure.

a *Chair Vise*

an *Apple Quarterer*

# To Sit at your Work . . .

Clamp block
("BLOCK-HEAD")
PIN
JAW
SEAT

the Shaving Horse

HOLES FOR ADJUSTING
TO DIFFERENT USES

foot lever
(WEIGHTED)

Apprentice Horse

PIN

block

SEAT

SEAT

weight

foot lever

Saw filing Horse
1850

about 1790

Nailer's Anvil Horse

35

The American saw-horse is now usually carpenter-made and hastily knocked together by the workman to be discarded "after the job is done"; it can also be bought ready-made, put together with "two-by-fours" and metal fasteners. Either way the modern saw-horse is more a temporary prop than a well-designed table. The early saw-horse, which had a flat top, was wide enough to hold the wood being sawed and other things too; it was usually a handy and permanent part of the tool room.

An Early American sawyer's prop was made of two clubs pushed against a raised log. A later arrangement was the "tackle prop," a stick pushed through a forked bough; two of these could hold a whole log in place.

The first "saw-buck" was a tripod (a tilted cross with a stick through it) and it was called a "saw-goat" instead of a "saw-buck" (the Dutch word *zaag-boc* means saw-goat). So the three-legged *zaag-boc* became our four-legged saw-buck!

Zaag-boc to Saw-buck 1600's — 1700's

# "Sawhorses" were saw-tables

**1750**

for carpenters...

or when **Logs** were to be sawed, you used a **Sawyer's Prop**

made of "two clubs"

or a **Sawing Tackle**

hole

Single or double

37

# For Making "Snitzels"

First called the "drawing knife" because you drew it toward you, the drawknife (or snitzel-knife, as some Pennsylvanians called it) came to America before the Pilgrims. But only with the emergence of the snitzel-bank, or shaving horse, which made it simpler to hold the article being shaved, did the drawknife become a most favored tool. There are probably more ancient drawknives extant than any other antique tool.

The drawknife was used to taper the sides of shingles, to rough-size the edges of floor boards and rough-trim paneling before planing them, to fashion axe, rake, and other tool handles, and to make stool legs, ox yokes, pump handles, and wheel spokes. It is easy to see why the drawknife was so popular! The final finishing on much drawknife work was done by our next tool, the spokeshave and scraper.

3"
Coachmaker's drawknife.
(there were many versions of this)

brass ferrules

a Jigger (or gigger)
combination straight & hollowing

# The Drawknife first called Draft Shave

ranged from the 24" **Mast Drawknife**

1840

to the 6" bladed <u>Cooper's Drawknife</u>.

bent-over tines
to secure the
handles.

about
1700

**Drawknife work was
done on the <u>Shaving Horse</u>**
... the piece worked on
clamped by the "Jaw"

... or done on a
<u>Shaving Block</u>, the piece held by
a <u>block hook</u> (and the worker's
body X)

STAVE

..... or for bench
work, a
<u>Screw cramp</u>

Hollow
shave

39

# Little Shavers and Big

The difference between the drawknife and its little brother the spoke-shave is like the difference between the old open razor and the safety razor. The spokeshave has a regulated depth of cut. Tap the tangs and the cut deepens; tap the face of the blade back and it becomes more shallow. Often a screw held the adjustment in place. All-metal spokeshaves appeared just before the Civil War; before that, the variety of wood handles seems endless.

The biggest shaver was the chamfer knife, sometimes all metal, which is often misrepresented (even by the experts) as a kind of froe. The sharp upper surface, however, shows that it was not designed for striking; and the curve-beveled blade is certainly not for splitting.

Although the tiny tools shown below were called "top and side shaves," they were really planes. They were designed for the use of stair-makers, but coachmakers found them even more useful.

Littlest shavers were
*Stair Planes*

Top Shave

3¾"

Hand rail

Side shave

The little **Spokeshave**

tang
blade

9½  viewed as from the eyes of the user
seen from below. **Here**
is a cross
section through
a spokeshave

tang

blade

tang

wood

BLADE

**Here is a bottom view** showing an added **Wear Plate**

ALSO CALLED
"HEEL" and
"SHOE"

P L A T E

B L A D E

TANG

TIGHTENING
SCREWS FOR
LOCKING BLADE
AT CORRECT
HEIGHT

REAR

TOP

the
Cooper's
Down
Shave

**The Chamfer Knife**

not flat

1850

metal
handle.

c. 1675

about 1750

# The Days of River Rafting

In many wooded areas of eighteenth-century America, farmers raised crops mostly for their own use and derived cash only from the sale of wood. Timber was floated to its destination by means of fastening logs into giant rafts. Three or more "platforms" were fastened, one behind the other, to make one long raft; steering was done by long oars. When rafts were sold and dismantled at the mill, irons and fastening devices were put into kegs, loaded on wagons, and hauled back to the farm. Most farmers ran at least one raft a year in late winter (when rivers were high) and busied themselves a good part of each winter with making or repairing lumbering implements.

White pine for masts and spars was a prime American export in the early 1800's and up until the Civil War. On such rivers as the Delaware were floated more than a thousand rafts each spring. The largest one on record was 215 feet long, and it contained 120,000 feet of lumber.

Below is a device known as a "bow-and-pin fastener." The square pins were driven into holes in the log; the wooden bow held the lash pole in place.

# a Connecticut River Timber Raft of 1820

one "platform" about 100 ft.

Lash Poles

a Snake Raft (sets of four logs "dogged" together.)

Raft Shackles

a Raft Dog

The Log Tongs for four men

The logger's "Pickaroon"

was often made from an axe head

the Ring Dog was a pocket-size cant hook for rolling logs.

12"

# Tools of the River Lumberman

*The American word "lumberman" came before our present
use of the word lumber. "Lumber" at one time (and still does in England)
meant "anything useless or cumbersome."*

The so-called "ship augers" you find in antique shops had not, as you
might think, anything to do with ships; they were really used for log-
rafts, or log-ships. The length of these augers allowed a man to bore a
hole while standing.

The lash-pole and wooden-pin method of building rafts was later re-
placed by iron raft shackles and "dogs."

Loose logs were "herded" into "corrals" by the owners at the mill
(branded with the owners' marks). The marking axe was also an inspec-
tion axe with a special bark-lifting poll.

Below you may see how the cant hook was made (in 1870 by a blacksmith named John Peavey) into the "American peavey" by wedding it to
the jam pike. The jam pike pried, the cant hook rolled, but the peavey
did both.

The *Cant Hook*
for rolling a log

iron spike

the *Jam Pike*

with the addition of
a *Cant Hook*, became

The *Peavey* 1871

# Raft Auger

for pinning
log-rafts
together with
saplings and
pegs. (X)

Logs
were
bored on
land, but
some experts
could do it
afloat.

X

Five feet

or with **Raft Shackles**
of chained
spikes

Logs were "stamped"
by a **Marking Axe**
with the initials of the owner

1810

Pick
for
lifting
bark.

ES

# Of Cider and Apple Butter

Anything that touched apples, according to the old way of thinking, had to be made of wood. Even a nail would "risk spoiling the flavor" or "quicken a souring." So heavy treen-ware (appliances and tools made from trees) was necessary in the apple industry.

Cider was never a matter of just squeezing—there was a special art to "bruising" apples and leaving them exposed to air for a certain and exact time before pressing. Oddly, those who picked eating apples carefully from the tree to avoid bumping them made an elaborate ceremony of crushing the same fruit when making cider.

Apples were never squeezed: "pomace was pressed." A mash was made into pomace or "cheese," then carefully placed between straw mats so the juice could be pressed out. The pomace rake, apple butter scoop, "cheese cutter," and apple shovel are tools that are difficult to understand now, for they are lost to the times when cider was America's national drink and apple butter the national spread.

Apple butter Scoop          1790

Combination Scoop and paddle (both Shaker)

Cider "cheese cutter"

Apple and Grain Shovels

3 ft.

of Maple, poplar basswood or tulip.

Apple Butter Paddles and Stirrers

PEG

Apple or sassafras heads

a Pomace rake

an Apple Barrow
1800

47

# To Remove Bark

Until recently the main source of tannin for treating hides was obtained from oak bark, and the production of oak bark was an essential part of the economy of many American farms. In April and May, bark peeled easily, and this was done with the spud, barking iron, and barking axe. The peeling chisel and adze were used mostly for "debarking" cedar posts and cleaning logs before broad-axing. The irons and spuds were true tanbark tools, usually blacksmith-made to order.

At first, chunks of oak bark were ground under massive stone mill wheels that turned into a trough of stone, but as early as 1797 the iron bark mill entered the scene to create a major American industry.

The liquor for tanning was obtained by pouring cold water on finely ground bark and leaving it to stand for a few days. Then it was passed from one leaching pit to another till the desired strength was reached.

to horse power

a Bark Mill 1797.

Bark enters here.
Casing (teeth inside).
Conical toothed Drum.

Tanbark

# Bark was stripped from logs with the Bark Spud

Stripping to hasten drying of timber wood

NEW ENGLAND C.1800

NEW YORK 1850

## and Peeling Chisel

## and Barking Irons

for cutting Bark for Tanning

1800's

spoon spud

harvested oak bark

about 1790

## The Barking Axe did the ringing

c.1730

SPUD.

and splitting before the Spud's work

3 FT.

# Two Heads are Better than One.

Except for the double-bitted axe, these tools are rare. So rare in fact, that there is doubt about their true names. One of the first dictionary mentions of the "twibil" calls it "an iron tool used by Paviers" (road-builders). This would make it a sort of grubbing hoe. Another describes it as a twin-billed hoe-and-knife for beans and peas. One old dictionary says the "twivel" is "among Carpenters, a tool to make Tortoise Holes." We must assume this definition was dictated to a printer who mistook "mortise" for "tortoise."

I would guess that all two-bitted hatchets might have been at some time called "twin-bills," "twibils," or "twivels." Still used in England to cut hurdle mortises, the twivel there is called "tomyhawk," "dader," or "two-bill."

The ice hatchet, adze-hatchet, and hatchet-adze were American, but only the Yankee double-bit remains. From Maine (about 1840) it was designed with one razor-sharp bit that could do fine work and one less sharp for rough work. It also provides a means for being held (by sinking it into a stump) for filing either bit.

the *Bec d'Ane*
(donkey-nose)
for rough
Mortises
c. 1780
c. 1700 or before
and *Tenons*
a two-angled striking chisel

The Twibil and Twivel

cutting a mortise with a Twivel

New England about 1650

STRUCK RARELY    MOSTLY SWUNG

with one or two hands

for making Mortises.

The Ice Hatchet

1780

the Adze-hatchet

and its opposite, the Hatchet-adze which became the Grubbing-axe.

1850

the American-designed Yankee Axe

chocked into a stump for sharpening with a file.

# The Chisel

There are so many kinds of chisels that it is difficult to establish definite nomenclature; yet, on the opposite page, we have attempted a general classification. The firmer (or firming or forming) chisel is the basic chisel design; it did a great many jobs, but one special use was to cut the superfluous wood from two auger holes to make a mortise. The framing chisel is a heavier version, and it was used largely in the cutting of tenons to fit the mortises. Both of these tools are wood-handled (usually socketed) and were designed to be struck with a mallet. The socket-end can be struck bare, without the handle, though a good craftsman seldom did this.

The short, stout mortise chisel is almost square, a one-purpose tool. The giant paring chisel, known as a slick, has a big blade that curves very slightly toward the bevel; it was designed, not for striking, but to be used with two hands (often with some shoulder help) like a giant plane. Big framing chisels are often misnamed slicks; if the curve is evident, it is a slick; if not, it is a giant framing chisel.

*Socket fitted*

*a Tang*

CUFF

*Generally, the tang was used on smaller chisels*

*The condition of the cuff on many old chisels, shows that much striking was done without use of the handle*

The **Firmer** or Forming Chisel was the all-purpose cutter.

more often Tanged

The **Framing** Chisel was for heavier jobs.

"**Mortise** chisel just cut a mortise.

the **Slick** was razor sharp, never struck but pushed by hands and shoulder.

also called Paring Chisel

2½" to 4½"

25" to 34"

Strong, short, deeply basilled

ALMOST SQUARE HERE

auger hole

the Firmer cut away superfluous wood. Mortise chisel cut directly. (Both made Mortises.)

2" to 4" wide Notice curve toward the bevel side

53

# Chisels and Gouges

What many call a "round chisel" is really a "gouge." The story told on the opposite page is that the earliest gouges were usually all metal (blacksmith-made from the Old World) and copied in this country in larger form for use with wooden handles.

The 1775 gouge in the illustration has an interesting story. It was found in a stone fence. Bright and silverish, its edge is keen; it has no rust. How farm-bound bog iron, privately smelted, hammered together at a farm forge, could be better in any way than today's steel is a mystery. I have compared the best chisels (the most expensive, that is) by leaving them in the rain alongside this ancient tool. The new tool's edge was dulled, and rust appeared within a few days.

The legend is that early surface ore contained much manganese and was purer in iron content. It is also believed that the use of charcoal gave purer carbon content and made a superior iron.

The chisels shown below had individual uses; some were used as bark scrapers, others as beam smoothers (like big planes). But I cannot find them listed or catalogued. Some ice chisels are similar, but they lack a tilted bit (see below—*x*).

*x*

this one was used in a clapboard mill

all iron

5"

wood

Specially made Chisels of the 1800's

# Connecticut Farm-made Gouge

notice <u>Nail</u> hammered
into the metal.
c.
1700

## Bowl Gouges

ALL METAL

WOOD

c.
1680

c.
1740

ALL METAL

c.
1775

c.
1675

## the Skew Chisel
a rare forming
chisel used in
mortise work

These mortise tools were at first, all metal.

① ②

ALL METAL

c.
1750

**Corner Chisel**

c.
1850

## Gooseneck
or "socket-lock Chisel"
began as a barn mortise
router, ended as a door
lock mortise tool ②

①

heel

# Planes

Old World planes, made as much to look at as to do a job, often had inscriptions and floral carving. But the completely utilitarian American plane, except for an occasional graceful handle, usually resembled a box. Looking alike, a nest of small planes in the average carpenter's chest often reached thirty or more. Perhaps because of their plainness, or their quantity, they never caught the collector's fancy. Not long ago in Vermont, you could buy them by the barrel as firewood for five dollars. That included the barrel!

From the big ones ("long" planes) down, these either leveled the surface or fit pieces (side by side) together. Leveling was called "trying" and "trueing"; fitting was called "jointing."

With the trying plane (top, opposite) was a smaller bench plane called a jack plane and a larger (now rare) mate, the long jointer, or floor plane. But all other planes bow to their granddaddy in size, the cooper's long jointer, which was used upside down on a pair of legs to work the piece. Restricted in use mostly to joining barrel staves, this plane sometimes had two blades—one for rough, one for fine cut.

a Favorite — Hand-made Plane,

Natural Handle of oak

"bit or Iron" made from an old file.

# The Long Planes ("Trying" for floors and roughing, and "Jointer" for joining)

iron or bit wedge

stock

toat

FOR APPRENTICE push stick

"Trying or trueing"

sole

Long jointer or Floor plane

← - - - - - - - - 3 ft. more or less - - - - - - - - →

## the Cooper's Long Jointer
### was used "upside down."

1600's

1700's

STAVE

. . . nearly 6 ft. long!

## Here are some general dimensions

| Names of Planes | length | width | iron width |
|---|---|---|---|
| Modelling Plane | 1" to 5" | ¼" to 2" | 3/16" to 1½" |
| Smoothing Plane | 6" to 8" | 2½" to 3½" | 1¾" to 2⅜" |
| Rabbet Plane | 9½" | 3/8" to 2" | 3/8" to 2" |
| Jack Plane | 12" to 17" | 2½" to 3" | 2" to 2¼" |
| Long or Trying Plane | 20" to 26" | 3½" | 2½" to 2⅝" |
| Jointer Plane or Floor Plane | 28" to 36" | 3¾" | 2¾" |
| Cooper's long jointer | 60" to 72" | 5" to 5½" | 3½" to 3¾" |

# The Moulding Plane

The grandest plane was the crown moulding plane. That large strip between the wall and ceiling was the identification of a fine room as well as the mark of the craftsman. No workman even carried about so large a tool and few owned one; instead the ordinary workman improvised with the basic "hollow" and "round" planes to make a moulding that the crown could do at one sweep.

The big crown plane was so heavy that it had bars for the apprentice to pull it by rope (1). Or, looped once or twice around a mill-wheel shaft (2), it could be pulled by tightening the rope, released by loosening.

Some crown planes had an apprentice pulling stick (3); others had a bar screwed across the front of the stock (4); others had two bars that slid into the front and back of the stock (5), with a notch for a second apprentice to push by stick.

The simplest moulding plane made a bead, but even this design came in sets of eight (from an eighth of an inch to a full inch), so you can see how a well-equipped carpenter's chest often had twenty or more moulding planes.

this

Littlest moulding plane puts a Bead

on a corner of a beam.

# The Moulding Planes

## Crown moulding

1835

①

②

ONE TURN AROUND
THE MILL WHEEL AXLE

7"

15"

Fence

THE FENCE KEPT
PLANE GOING STRAIGHT.

With help of apprentice (1) — or mill-power (2) a wide moulding
could be cut at once. But the **Hollow** and **Round**
could do
a good job
too

a
*Hollow* Plane
(Also called a *Fork Staff*.)

a
*Round*
plane

a *Moulding*
*"Pull Plane"*   ③

for apprentice
help

④

⑤

Notch for Push-stick.

# The Rabbet

Most American carpenters call it a "rabbit"; the British call it a "rebate." It is really the "rabbet plane" that "rabbets" out a cut in the sides of boards, so that they may be overlapped and joined. This was the popular way of joining before milled tongue-and-groove.

The first rabbet and the long rabbet plane have fences (overlapping strips) to guide the plane along the end of the board (as shown on the opposite page). Because the little rabbet stands flat without a fence, it needs a strip of wood nailed along its route to guide it before it can properly cut a rabbet in a board.

These planes vary in design, some throwing shavings to the right, some to the left, some to both sides. Some irons have blades set, instead of at a right angle, on a skew to the stock to avoid tearing the wood. Rarer is the pistol-grip-handled rabbet, which lacks the usual wedge for holding the iron. Below is the rabbet saw, rarely used except in stairmaking.

a variation of the stair-saw,
a rabbet could be cut with a

*Rabbet saw*

C. 1860

adjustable
fence

The Rabbet Plane — made a corner groove

wedge

STOP IRON FENCE

WOOD

a Long Rabbet

B.J.S. 1860

FENCE

and

iron from long rabbet plane

a small rabbet

and iron

c. 1780

The early Rabbets were handled or flat and very "wide-eyed"

screw through iron

Eye

throat

a Double Rabbet corner

14"

lapping Rabbets

F.S.T. 10        c. 1810

a Half Rabbet corner

# The Plow

The plow plane did the simplest job, yet it looks like the most complicated of tools. It just makes a groove. We use tongue-and-groove cuts for flooring and sheathing without realizing how recent this practice is. Before the "tongue" was popular, two grooves were placed against each other, and a "spline" was driven into the "tunnel" to join the two pieces together. For paneling, a tongue was not planed, but a "feather edge" was set into the groove.

The adjustable plow had its fence attached to the plane by two arms that slid through the plane stock and made secure by wooden wedges. Later the square arms became two long round screws with threaded knobs to hold them secure.

The unadjustable plow and unadjustable tongue plane came in pairs ("tongue-and-groove sets"), and there was also a combination of the two, set into one stock (see following pages).

## Uses of the Plow Plane in joining wood

Plowed and Cross-tongued

"Spline," "tongue" or "feather."

Feather-edged

FRAME

PANEL

Door-Panel (flush on one side)

Drawer-Plowed

drawer bottom

# The Plow Plane ...made a Groove along the end of a board

Simplest Plow... with thin iron plate

...but the Adjustable Fence Plow (first wedged, later screwed) are best-known types.

1790

FENCE

(Shown head on)

BIT — GROOVE

1850

WOODEN SCREWS

# The Adjustable Plow ...as seen from below.

Notice how slide-arms slide through the stock (x)

wedge

X

wedge

X

a Plowing Iron

bit

Fence

# PLANES,

## FOR
## CARPENTERS, COOPERS, CABINET AND COACH MAKERS.

| | CAST STEEL. Single. | CAST STEEL. Double. | IRONS. GERMAN STEEL. Single. | IRONS. GERMAN STEEL. Double. | | CAST STEEL. Single. | CAST STEEL. Double. | IRONS. GERMAN STEEL. Single. | IRONS. GERMAN STEEL. Double. |
|---|---|---|---|---|---|---|---|---|---|
| Jointers 30 inch | $1 70 | $2 17 | $1 58 | $2 05 | Cooper's Jointers | $2 50 | $3 50 | $2 88 | $3 88 |
| do 28 " | 1 64 | 2 09 | 1 52 | 1 96 | do stock howel | 2 50 pl'd | 3 00 | 2 38 | 2 88 |
| do 26 " | 1 58 | 2 00 | 1 46 | 1 88 | do circ. leveler | 1 50 " | 2 00 | 1 38 | 1 87 |
| do 22 " | 1 50 | 1 92 | 1 38 | 1 80 | do with handles | 2 00 | 2 50 | 1 88 | 2 38 |
| do 21 " | 1 42 | 1 84 | 1 30 | 1 72 | do crows | 2 50 | | | |
| Jack Planes | 96 | 1 37½ | 88 | 1 30 | Tooth Planes | 1 25 | | | |
| Smooth Planes | 87½ | 1 25 | 80 | 1 17 | Miter Planes | 1 00 | | | |
| do Circular | 92 | 1 31 | 84 | 1 23 | Ogees for Cabinet Makers, $1 00 per inch. | | | | |

| | | | | |
|---|---|---|---|---|
| Astragals ⅛ to ½ inch | | 62½ | Match Planes, fence plated | 3 00 |
| do ⅝ to 1 inch | | 75 | do moving fence | 4 00 |
| Beads ⅛ to ⅜ inch | | 75 | do screw arms | 6 00 |
| do over 1 inch | | 67½ | Plows, 1st rate, 8 irons | 7 00 |
| do full boxed ⅛ to ⅜ | | 92 | do 2d " " | 6 00 |
| do do ½ to ⅞ | 1 00 | | do 3d " " | 5 00 |
| Coves to ⅜ inch | | 62½ | do 4th " " | 4 50 |
| do ⅜ to 1 inch | | 75 | Extra for boxing fence | 50 |
| Cove and Beads ⅜ to ½ inch | | 75 | Extra for side screws | 50 |
| do do ⅝ to 1 inch | | 87½ | do screw arms and 8 irons | 7 00 |
| do do over 1 inch | 1 00 | | do box fence | 7 50 |
| Center Beads to ⅜ | | 87 | do side screws | 8 00 |
| Dadoes, slide stop | | 1 37 | do solid box | 8 00 |
| do screw stop | | 2 00 | do do side screws | 8 50 |
| Fillisters | | 1 50 | Rabbet Planes to 1 inch square 62, skew | 75 |
| do with stop | | 1 75 | do 1¼ inch 68, skew | 87½ |
| do do and cut | | 2 00 | do 1½ inch 75, skew | 92 |
| do do cut and boxed | | 2 25 | do 1¾ inch 78, skew | 1 00 |
| do with screw stop, cut and boxed | | 3 00 | do 2 inch | 1 12½ |
| Guages | | 20 | do with handles | 2 00 |
| do oval head | | 25 | Extra for boxing | 25 |
| Gothic Beads | | 1 25 | Extra for adding cut | 25 |
| Grecian Ovolos ⅜ by ⅜ inch | | 1 00 | Raising Planes, common | 1 75 |
| do do ½ by 1 inch, ⅝ by 1¼ | | 1 12½ | do moving fence | 3 25 |
| do do ⅞ by 1½ inch | | 1 25 | do do 3 in. iron | 4 00 |
| do do Beads ⅝ by ⅜ in., ½ by 1¼ in. | | 1 25 | do do 3½ " | 4 50 |
| do do ⅞ by 1¾.—⅝ by 1¼ inch | | 1 50 | do do 4 " | 5 00 |
| do do do ⅞ by 1¾ and 2 inch | | 1 75 | Reeding Planes ⅛ to ½ inch | 1 00 |
| do Ogee and Bevel sq. ⅞ by ⅜ in., ⅝ by 1⅛ in. | | 1 25 | Sash Planes, 1 iron 1 00, boxed | 1 50 |
| do do do ⅝ by 1⅜ in., ⅞ by 1½ in. | | 1 50 | do 2 " 1 50, " | 2 00 |
| do do do ⅞ by 1¾ and 2 inch | | 1 75 | do double 2 50, " | 3 00 |
| Halving planes | | 62½ | Snipe Bills | 75 |
| do do plated | | 87½ | do full box | 1 00 |
| do do with handles | | 1 00 | Side Rabbets | 62½ |
| do do plated, with handles | | 1 25 | Torus Beads to ⅜ inch | 75 |
| Hollows and Rounds 9 pair to No. 18. | | 10 50 | do from ⅜ to 1 inch | 87½ |
| Match Planes for Boards ⅝ to 1 inch | | 1 75 | do over 1 inch | 1 00 |
| do fence plated | | 2 00 | Table Planes, pair | 1 50 |
| do for Plank 1¼ inch | | 2 62½ | do boxed | 2 00 |

*Omitting various moulding planes and special planes (such as those illustrated on the opposite page), the above advertisement of the 1800's lists some of the basic planes that the average carpenter was likely to have in his chest. As many of these planes came in sets of eight, the army of old-time wooden planes seems overwhelming.*

a *Gallery of Planes Unusual.*

Horned Rabbet

Two-blade Rabbet

FOR LEFT OR RIGHT HAND

a Chisel-plane

Scooper Plane
FOR SCOOPS, SHOVELS ETC.

Carriage-Maker's Plane

C. 1840

Tongue-and-Groove

Groove (plow)
Tongue

FOR SCRATCHING A SURFACE BEFORE GLUEING

Toothing plane

Compass Plane

Carver's Rabbet
only 3" long

the Sun-plane
for levelling barrel-tops

# Early American Saws

Both the frame saw and the open saw were in use during the first American settlements. The open saw is very much like its modern counterpart, but it had a handle like that of a knife and it was long enough to be used by two hands. Americans enjoyed using wood in their tools, and the wooden frame saw was most popular. Metal was hard to come by, and the frame saw had the advantage of needing only the narrowest blade.

Saw nomenclature is uncertain, but the most common division is that of "open" and "frame" types. The bow saw (again a frame type) was stretched taut between two arms by a twisted cord (or by rod and screw); the saw blade was readily turned by twisting the handles, making it easy to saw curved pieces.

The buck saw is a bow frame type, but its blade is stationary and heavier, and a long handle has been added. To "buck" logs was to saw them into proper lengths; hence, the buck saw is a woodsman's saw.

winding stick
Brace
arms
Collapsible!
the rigid blade and Handle makes it a Buck Saw

# The Open Saw

Handle
for one or both
hands
c. 1740

"nicked"
## Farm saw
made from an old
scythe blade.

tang
mounted

## Tenon Saw
c. 1800

2 ft.

ROOT

tang and
rivets. (c. 1700)

note
ornament

x
x

x

## Anglo-American
### Factory
blades with hand-made handles.

tang
rivets
these are
1750's or earlier

after 1760

# The Frame Saw

5 ft.
Two man
Coach-
maker's
Saw

wedge

blade
4" to 5"

for planks
and
heavy stock

same style but a
thinner blade, the
## Veneer Saw
blade only
1" to 2"

screw

## the Bow
Saw was
stretched
across one end
of the frame ...
the blade was
turned
by

x

x

twisting
the
handle (x)

the Bow
is tightened
by a cord ...
or by a rod
and screw

bow

tightening
screw

67

# a Gallery of Frame Saws

The frame saw looks clumsy to us now, but actually it was much more of "an extension of the craftsman's hand" than the modern saw. You can cut straight or around corners with it and always see where the blade was cutting. The modern saw blade is wide, always covering the spot it is cutting, and is restricted to a straight cut.

The terms "chairmaker's saw," "felloe (also "felly") saw," "turning saw," etc. are difficult to pin to one model because each design overlapped the other in size or shape at one time or another. The frame saw is "strained" in the center and two stretchers keep it taut; the bow saw is strained on one end, with a stretcher cord (or rod) on the other.

The finer the work to be done the finer the saw; some frame saws are pieces of art both to work with and to look at.

*Nothing crude about the bow saw!*

oak

yew

walnut

hickory
maple

extra handle

# Frame Carpenter's Saw (bow)
did general work.

## Chairmaker's Saw
had thinner blade; it cut curves.. same

as the

## Felloe saw

CHAIR SEAT

WHEEL

Here, handle has twisted blade to right angle

(a Felloe is a segment of a wheel)

## Bow-Felloe
and
## Frame-Felloe Saw.

PIN

Blade connection on a bow saw

Blade connection on a frame saw

SLOTTED SHAFT

PIN

about 1/2"

30"

# The Biggest Saws

Its teeth raked to cut downward, the long pit saws (both open and framed) did most of the earliest American plank-sawing both from trestles and in pits. The open type was more recent in the New World than the framed model. Factory-made, the open pit saw was used until the late 1800's.

*There was an ancient open plank saw (see below) that some collectors regard as an open pit saw, but the curved blade and matching handles indicate otherwise.*

an *Ancient Open Plank-saw* (c. 1600)

*not like our pit saw.*

Marks of an Up-and-down Saw-Mill saw

Marks of a Pit Saw

(Finer and at an Angle)

the *Open Pit Saw*

Tiller Man

the *Frame Pit Saw*

Box Man

*Trestle*

*Pit*

*the box man wore a big hat because of the shower of sawdust*

The Open Pit Saw and the Frame Pit Saw

tiller

C.
1800

c.
1750

7'

"Box"

wedge

71

# to Make a Hole

Although awls seem no more than sharp points with handles, there are those who collect them as basic tools. The awl and punch enter wood by "spreading" the fibers apart; the ream, auger, and gimlet "cuts." The "burn auger" (1) was fired to a red-hot point that burned its opening in the wood; then it was twisted to make the hole deeper. The "wood punch" (2) was hammered into the wood, and was twisted both for deeper cut and for release. The "ream awl" (3) had sharp corners that acted as cutting agents.

The "gouge bit" (split-quill) was round-ended, like a gouging chisel; if water was put into its cavity it would run out the end. If water was dropped into a "spoon bit" or "pod auger," it would stay in, for the nose of the bit scoops upward into a twist (A and B). The "twisted cylinder" bit, neither podlike nor triangular, has parallel sides, one of which is a cutting edge. The cutter of the nose auger is shown below, along with the same device on a spiral-ribbon bit.

Down-cutting bit on a Nose Auger

...and on a Spiral Auger

CUTTING EDGE

UNDERNEATH and SIDE VIEW, SHOWING CUTTING LIP

the
Burn Auger

Wood Punch

Ream
Awl

(1.)

(2.)

(3.)

a Burning-awl
burning out a
Sumac Spile
for maple sap

Quill
Gimlet

2 1"

Twisted
Gimlet
(1½ turns)

Pod Auger

"Gouge Bit"
"Split-quill", "reed"

"Spoon Bit"
"Duck-bill", "dowel-bit"

"Nose Auger"
(DOWN-CUTTING BIT)
"table-cutter" nose bit
(see page to left).

"Twisted Cylinder"
(REALLY HALF-CYLINDER).

"Pod-Bit"
Ⓐ
Ⓑ
with screw (A) and knife (B) points

# To Make a Hole Bigger

To enlarge a hole, you may "ream" it with a tapered blade; to be sure, the hole will be tapered too, but often (as when you are cutting a barrel bung-hole or a wheel hub-hole) this is just what you want. The biggest of all reamers is the wheelwright's hub reamer; often it reaches a length of three feet and weighs as much as twenty-five pounds. Some of these can still be found without handles and with strange hooks. Oddly enough, the experts have not decided just how these were used. But I rigged up a wagon wheel on a wheelwright's bench, then put a hooked reamer through the hub, which I had weighted with seventy-five pounds. With two men turning a very long detachable handle (which might explain the missing handles on so many of these blades it worked nicely). With an ordinary reamer, a man exerts about half his weight downward; this can be bettered with a seventy-five-pound weight plus the twenty-five-pound weight of the tool itself.

Tap augers and hub reamers were usually sharpened on one blade (on the inner side).

an early type Tapering Bore

2 ft.

C. 1750.

12"

c 1850.

Spiral edge Taper Auger

The Tap Auger (one hand)
cut a tapered hole : so did
the two·handed model

but the
Wheelwright's
Reamer

enlarged
hub·holes

_and so
did the
Hooked
Reamer

7"

2 ft.

Hub

Wheel·
wrights
Bench

and

A possible method of using the
Hooked Reamer

75 lb.
weight

3 ft.

Hook

x

# to Make a Bigger Hole

Recently a "revolutionary speed bit" was introduced for electric drills. Actually it is an adaptation of an early "button bit" (A) and (B) and has the same design as the "center bit" (c. 1794) with which the pioneer American started trunnel holes in his buildings. For shallow holes or to start a boring, it cut downward without pulling shavings upward as the big spiral bit does. Center bits, therefore, which were never put on bar handles, were used with a brace.

The four typical wooden bar handles shown are generalizations; because so many men made their own handles, it is difficult to pinpoint the date of a handle from its design. I have worked out these estimates, from the handles in my own collection, in the hope that this information might be helpful in dating tools in other collections.

It seems incredible that a man could turn the huge bits that some augers have. The job was made easier in the 1800's by a two-handled drill (shown opposite); an adjustable model came out in the 1860's that drilled at any angle.

"Blacksmith-made twist bit with one blade (X) (c. 1800)

then two blades

...then four blades

Never mounted on a Cross-bar handle like this

**The Center Bits**

cut downward only and did not pull shavings upward.

Router    Scriber

A      B

TWO BLADES    ONE BLADE

Cutter     AT WORK

Primitive bar handle
c. 1650 to 1790

c. 1750 to 1840

middle 1800's

after 1850

**The Boring Machine**

... made mortising easy.
Two holes, chiselled easily
into a mortise

1.     2.

Operator sat here and
turned the machine with both hands.

# The Brace or Bitstock

The early American bitstock or brace was made of native seasoned hard-wood. Some of the earliest were made of natural-shaped roots or boughs (see drawing in center, opposite page). Oak and hickory were most commonly used although the burl-wood bitstock was also prized.

Most early braces (particularly in New England) were "bitted" in a permanent manner; the bit was moulded into a metal wad and fitted tightly into a square wooden chuck (sometimes ferruled), and this square chuck was wedged into the stock to stay.

The revolving buttons were masterpieces of woodworking, for most of those on the earliest braces still work nicely and are not even cracked. The button was either "stayed" by a wooden pin through the shaft and head (A), or the shaft was "stayed" by a "Cotter-pinlike" peg (B). The natural-shape stock's button was loose, staying in just by pressure. (As some braces were rested against the chest—and therefore needed a bigger and flatter button—this brace may have had interchangeable buttons, one for the hand and one for the chest.)

The "Cage Head" of a Coachmaker's Brace
Connecticut c.1750

this large head was for resting against the chest

this screw appeared c.1720

Button

A

Natural Shape

LOOSE BUTTON

Elbow

PIN

B

C 1775 N.Y.

Maine c. 1725

oak

iron ring

Lead cuff

ferrule

This bit and chuck were fastened in (not made removable).

Center bit

Philadelphia c. 1765

pin

23"

wedge →

wooden
wedge

for bit

Metal chuck

an All-Wood
bitstock
with a
"Pumpkin
Handle"

wedge—

shaft—

lead
wad

oak
stock,
heat-
seasoned

Massachusetts...
c. 1730

the *Chuck* is wooden, locked in
place with a wedge....

... the *Bit* is bedded in tightly, in
early American
style

# The THINGS you'll find in a Barn!

One of the most popular pages of the monthly publication of a tool collectors' club is its "Whatsis Column." Antique gadgets that stump the experts are frequently turning up. In the era of hand-made tools, it was logical that one-of-a-kind implements were created—the man who custom-made his own tools could allow himself the luxury of making tools to meet *his* needs. Then, too, there were devices that had many uses. Ladders were used as tobacco driers; the bars of a ladder-back chair held candleholders; meat hooks doubled as grappling hooks that retrieved things from the bottoms of wells. If you think it strange that a hook was so necessary to a household, remember that the well was used many times a day, that foods needing refrigeration were often lowered into it. Items lost beneath the water could not, of course, be seen, so they could be retrieved only by groping. The well hook was used as much as any other implement of the old-time household. After all, who wanted to drink water from a well filled with old pails?

These tiny Hammers were not Carpenters':
they were hung on sleds.... They knocked snow
from horses' hoofs.

all iron    5½"    called Yankee Snow Knockers

two-piece
forged
*Well
Hook*

*A twisted model and a
One-
Piece
Hook* c
1770

c.
1830

*lifted pies
from ovens*

1800's

*a Pie Peel*

*Quarryman's
Mud Spoon*

(DIPPED STONE-DUST
FROM DRILLED HOLES)

*for a
wire*

*Cheese slicer*

*to loosen food from a
barrel, you used a*

*"Sugar-devil" or
Fruit Auger*

c.
1845

*a Snow Knocker*

*made to clip onto harness.*

*This hook could
serve many purposes. It was for candles.*

# Some were Special

Although nails and hooks and tacks and hundreds of other iron implements were hammered out by farmers all over the countryside, it was recognized as fitting that each item have its own sizes and patterns. The nails made in Maine look quite like the nails made in New Jersey, both in proportions and design; only an expert can tell a difference. People were religious about conforming to tradition; they had a profound reverence for accepted design that we nowadays feel is decadence.

Here are a few things that are of the past that you might find in old attics or barns, each thing for a special use. The stock-knife shaped wood, the mill pick dressed millstones, the barrel-scrape cleaned out barrels, the "commander" pushed beams "home" and into their mortises.

When I was trying to move a barn, I found a "commander" of better use than two men working with sledgehammers, and was pleased to see it sending beams into place without disfiguring them as the iron sledges did.

a Ceiling Hook for hanging things to dry.

a Skewer Hook

18"

"Drift Hook" really not a hook!

.. a temporary pin for testing wooden framework; to be knocked out by "up-hammering" at x.

The Stock-Knife - also called Block-Knife

1815

fastened to a block, it cut out rough wood shapes for the woodworking shop

WOOD HANDLE

a stock-knife unearthed at Jamestown, Va.

The Mill Pick

another type

"dressed" the buhr stone

the Commander was swung between the legs

Barrel-Scrape or "Scorp"

MORTISE and TENON

to pound beams "home" before raising.

STEP

Bog Root Cutter

1750

# These were Tools too!

"Sleds" were for winter; "sledges" were used year round. Tools the sledges were. If you would wish to learn the value of the sledge, try putting an ordinary house broom beneath a heavy trunk or object you wish to move. With someone then lifting one end, a child can easily pull the broom and its load across the floor. Farmers pulled unbelievable loads (on wooden runners) across grass on which a wheel would have sunk and become impossible. We know of the "stone boat," but the Early American farmer had a number of other sledge-type devices before the wheelbarrow. A sledge could be pulled by horse or ox through forest, and over rocks and onto the farm in winter ice or spring mud, whereas a wheeled vehicle could not. A wheeled vehicle is higher off the ground; this makes it inconveniently high for lifting loads *into* and it does tip over easily. So, harvesting and haying and moving rocks, dung, maple syrup barrels, etc. was done by sledge rather than wagon.

Here you may see a few of these early sliding devices. It might be safely said that for every wagon on the Early American farm, there were three to ten sledges. Even the hand-pulled model, like that shown below, was used until the early 1800's.

Even after horse and wagon vehicles, the *Tumbril Sledge* remained as a handy farm tool.

1650

a Two·man sledge

handle

late 1700's

a Harvest Sledge

half· round split pole

1780

a Log Sledge

half·round Beech runner.

a Barrow Sledge

an all purpose "Bob"

Sapling runner

87

# Jacks

The Early American was an artist at lifting and moving heavy objects. Foundations and stone fences were built with the lever principle and a few gadgets as well as with the help of oxen. Experts are often stumped by the strange hooks and loops of iron with teeth in them that are found in old barns. But these were blacksmith-made jack hooks for moving beams and logs and stones. The lever was any handy tree limb; the longer, the more leverage.

The "wagon jacks" you find in antique shops were used for many purposes. Carpenters, framers, blacksmiths, and wheelwrights included these jacks in their list of shop tools. Some of them are made entirely of wood (usually ash or hickory); and they have outlasted many automobile jacks that have rusted away and ended in the junk pile while the wooden jacks are as good as they were a century ago.

The Jack Hook used any handle suited to the work.

Rock — either a Loop, Hook, or Tongs

Lifted onto a roller, stones could be moved easily. or rolled off so:

stone — LEVER — by one man

c. 1780
*Pennsylvania Wagon Jack*

mechanism enclosed in two slabs of hollowed plank

the *Fence Jack*

stays

lifted rails or stones into fence positions.

longer handle, more lift

*New England Wagon Jack*
had sliding grip

*Roxbury Stage*

"Eccentric Wheel" *Stagecoach Jack* 1858.

*Maine Carriage Jack*

c. 1830

all wood

*Wagon Lift*

1700's

# The Blacksmith

"Smith" from "smite," "black" from "black metal" (as distinguished from silversmith brightwork), the "blacksmith" was the Early American handyman. He made nails, hinges, sled runners, anchors, scythes, hoes, utensils, axes, hooks, and every kind of tool. In the middle 1800's he began taking over the farrier's work of horseshoeing; till then the farrier was veterinary too.

Blacksmith tool design has not changed very much except for the hazelwood withes that held all upper tools (chisels and swages). Hardly an implement or utensil cannot be traced to the early blacksmith.

Some early Anvils. — the Stake anvil for sheet metal and light work

nail headers

c. 1740

Colonial Anvil

with nail-making hollows

c. 1650

horn

heel

Hardy

c. 1800

Swage Hammer

Farrier's Hammers

PEEN

POLL

EYE

FACE

Blacksmith's Hammers

**Beak Irons**

*into anvil*

**Rounding Tools**
"swages"

a **Withe**
of wetted
hazel-rods

"top tool"
was held by
a withe,

"bottom tool"

went
into anvil.

Chisel

withe

a **Spring Swage**

**Flat Bit**    **Crook Bit**    **Hammer Tongs**    **Hoop tongs**    **Round & Square Bits**

**Coupler "Reins"**

shoulder rest

**Farrier's Tools**

**Hoof Knives**

**Butteris**
(hoof-parer)
-- also buttress.

**Farrier's long chisel**

short chisel

**Pincers**

# Wrought Nailmaking

MACHINE-CUT      WROUGHT

Lacking in beauty, the "nail header" is hardly a collector's prize, yet its plainness does not adequately explain its infrequent appearance in antique shops. Considering how farmers made nails by the thousands during winter months around the forge or fireplace, the rarity of headers is a mystery.

Machine-cut nails taper only on two sides; wrought nails on four. The most common "rose nail" had four hammer hits (if done by an expert); the head of the "clasp nail" had sharp downward sides to cut into the surface; "plancher nails" had T-shaped heads to hold down flooring; the "scupper" nailed leather (as for a bellows). Though our "brad" is a small-headed nail, the word once meant "broad" and the "brad" was such a nail for planks.

Rose sharp   Rose flat   Clasp   Horse   Plancher (FLOORING)   Brad (L-HEAD)

CHISEL POINT

T head CLASPED

Lath

Scupper

a Nailer's Forge

weight

nail rods

# Nail Headers (bores)

7"

Pointed end
of nail rod was
cut by

NAIL
ROD

a *Hardy*

then put
into the
header

a *Spring Header*

FOR NAILS & RIVETS

to be
clamped
in a vise.

spring
effect

a *Nailer's Anvil*

Hardy or
"*Hack Iron*"

Bow attached
to ceiling.

the *Oliver* anvil

anvil

Foot
treadle

nail
rods

a *Nailer's Anvil Bench*

# Tanners and Curriers

A currier did *not* curry horses. His craft was to scrape and soften the rough hides after the tanner had treated them. The tanner's tools, so wet and messy when being used, were seldom things of beauty, but their lines were traditional and graceful. The tanner's knives had delicate curves to fit the curve of the tanner's beam.

The currier's beam was flat, just as his knife was. The shaving knife (also called beamer or head-knife) had a soft steel blade with its fine edge burred over (recurved) into a minute scraper form. This delicate edge needed constant turning with a "turning steel" and lifting with a "finger steel," which was kept handy between two fingers as the beamsman worked. (This recurved edge will have disappeared from wear and corrosion on ancient tools.)

Farmers made their own leather for shoes, hinges, and harness, so old barns often have such tools about.

Currier's Beam

Slickers

HARD WOOD "BEAM BOARD"

45"

stone

steel

Currier's Turning Steel
Currier's Finger Steel

CROSS SECTION THROUGH CURRIER'S KNIFE-BLADE

The Tanner's Unhairing Knife c. 1790

blade cross sections:

The Tanner's Fleshing Knife (concave)

A

B

cross section: ____ Two-edged: (A) FOR TRIMMING, (B) FOR SCRAPING

a Beamsman at work on a Tanner's Beam

c. 1720

c. 1860

The Currier had a flat beam to work on (see opposite page) and a Currier's Knife

"Shaving on the Beam"

(X)

A FINE RECURVED EDGE ("WIRE-EDGE")

EDGE KEPT TRIM WITH A "FINGER STEEL" (X)

# About Wheels

Early wheelwright tools were not much different from those of hard-wood joinery except for those shown here. The process of putting a wheel together is illustrated below. The tire (iron outer rim) was made by the blacksmith. After the tire was made hot in a bed of ashes, it was applied to the wooden wheel, and then cooled quickly. The contraction tightened the tire, and held the whole wheel together with a tremendous force.

1. *Hubs* (naves) were cut → and *augered* (to help drying)    Left with bark on, 2 to 8 years to *Season*    ←—about 16"—→

2. dried nave was *Turned* to a *hub-shape*    LATHE

3. *Hub is mortised to receive spokes*    (Spokes were made of oak, seasoned over 4 yrs.)

4. *Spokes are hammered in* and "*DISHED*" by spoke-set gauge in a    spoke → (A)    HUB    "*Wheelwright's Pit*"

5. *Felloes* were fitted to spokes on the Wheelwright's Bench, and there Planed, shaved, checked ready for tiring at the Blacksmith.    F E L L O E    dowel hole    dowel

# Wheelwright's Benches

Screw fastened to floor

c. 1800

Cask type

Penn. c. 1790

a Hub Cradle

FOR MORTISING HUB FOR SPOKES

The Traveler measured the tire Ⓐ

a Wing Compass

wedges

wing

another wedge fastening

after measuring the wheel which it must fit.

Ⓐ

FELLOE

surface of wheel

a Spoke Dog

1.

2.

pulled spokes into place.

# It's all in the Way you Hit it.

Today we think a hammer is a hammer—the same thing that lays a roof, cracks a nut! But the early craftsman (like a good golfer) knew that *how* you hit and *what you hit with* could make a difference in the job being done. See, in the drawing below, how the flail separates the grain while the pestle grinds it; yet both tools hit.

The "flinting pick" did the job of making gun flints; the "bricklayer's hammer" and "axe" and "raker" did work that is still admired after two centuries. The "printing mallet" stamped designs on painted floor cloths (popular before linoleum). The "flood gate hammer" didn't smash the gate; its massive weight just moved it. The "zax" cut roofing slate and made nail holes in it. The "trunnel hammer" knocked trunnels in without smashing them. And so on. Each "hammer" hit a special kind of blow to do the specialty the craftsman needed done.

To grind, break open, soften, pulverize ... you hit in different ways.

this **Pestle** was lashed to a springy *bough* and brought down just hard enough with these handles →

*Mortar*

"souple"

the **Flail** hit just right to separate the seed from the chaff.

"Hand staff"

swivel "Hood"

LEATHER THONGS →

DETAIL OF FLAIL HEAD

Flinting Pick
for making
Gun Flints.

10"

Bricklayer's
Hammer

1840

Brick
Axe

Raker

(IT
KNOCKED
OUT OLD
CEMENT)

Printing Mallet
for floor-cloth
designs

1850

Ice Axe

C. 1870

nail hole pick

an early
Tack Hammer

C.
1860

Double-clawed
Shaker Hammer

(SECOND CLAW LIFTED HIGHER)

Knife

Turn-Shoe Hammer

FOR ROUNDING
SHOE
LEATHER

C. 1780

Zaxes
for
slate

Burl
Hammer
for
Wood
Pins
(TRUNNELS)

Mold
board

a
Grist Mill Flood Gate Hammer

25 lbs.

99

# Hay Implements

Among the more plentiful old barn relics is the hay knife. Wide, heavy and with the blade on the outer edge, most people wonder how hay could be reaped with it. It didn't reap—it cut out portions of hay from the haystack. The hay-spade and hay-saw did the same thing. The hay-spade knife, however, doubled as pumpkin cutter in the days when pumpkins were animal food. Pumpkin stalks tended to choke animals, so pumpkins were cut from the top and the stalks destroyed.

The slender, sharp reaping hook became an American design of rare beauty by the late 1700's. But during the late 1800's the art of cutting gave way to the art of slashing, and a sickle is a better slasher. The earliest corn knife was machetelike, but the sicklelike corn knife appeared in the early 1800's.

The sickle reaped with the aid of a grass crook (hay crook), which was also used for pulling loose hay from the stack.

Although such serrations are usually worn away in ancient tools, the early sickles were usually serrated; this sets them apart from the slender reaping hook.

This Connecticut *Hay Knife* worked like a saw. c. 1850

*Hay Knives* didn't reap hay.. they cut into the haystack.

New England
*Hay Knives*
c.1780

cutting edge

c.1840

a
Spade
type

38"

step

Pennsylvania

c.
1850
*Corn Knife*
also used
for
*Tobacco*
cutting.

c.
1830

c
1760

this
is a
*Reaping Hook*
Graceful, slender,
no serrations

B

A

*Sickles* (A, B)
were smaller,
often notched.

a
*Hay Crook*

3 ft.

# Knives and Grass

The first American grass blades were from England and matched to naturally bent "snaths" (handles) without "nibs" (hand grips). Our early scythes and cradle scythes were things of rare grace. Even those of the 1800's that were factory-made retained the lines that made them different from the cruder European and English implements. The snath was usually made of willow, shaped in hot oil; the nibs and fingers of hickory; the sned of ash. Wire rods were added in the late 1800's.

The scythes and forks of America before the late 1800's will someday be prized as pieces of art, but as of now they are so large or cumbersome that few choose to collect them. You are almost never likely to see an ancient wooden rake or scythe broken, although those made during the last seventy-five years or so have an average life of about five to ten years.

Natural Two-prong Fork (often 6 ft. long)

Butternut wedges, riveted in.

Four-prong Hay Fork    late 1800's

Six-prong Hay Fork    Penn. c. 1840

riveted "grasp"

metal tips

Bull Rake or Hay Drag

NO RIB

a Sith Hook
c. 1650

shoulder
strap,
no nib.

a Four-finger "Bow"
Cradle

sned

fingers

3-finger.
Cradle

early
mowing
Scythe
c.
1750

earliest scythes
had one
nib or
none.

Bent
Hickory
grass
Scythe

Connecticut
c. 1780

made by
blacksmith

a
naturally
formed
Snath*

* (also called
snid and
sneath)

# Found in the Barn

Oddities now, common items a century ago, here are a few things that were found in old barns and brought to me for identification. A tiny yoke for a goose, a cheesemaker's curd cutter and stirrer, a big winnowing scoop one used to throw flailed grain into the air to let the wind blow away the chaff—these are things that bring the past back vividly. Most old barns have eel spears tucked away near the rafters, although there may not be a river or lake for miles around. Yet a century ago men prized their swamp and wetlands, and stored up water in millponds for waterpower instead of bulldozing over the wet places as we do now.

The American countryside was very different a century or two ago!

These iron things (Tangs) held "Nibs" (hand grips) on scythe handles. NIB

a Tool to twist straw or hay into Rope or cord... a "twiner" or "throw-crook" for binding grain and cornstacks

Barley Forks c. 1860 "thumb" thumb

Barn Lantern for a candle.

wooden Swingling Knives (FOR FLAX)

These wooden Pokes kept animals from jumping through fences.

These are for curds.

hung from neck

this one for Geese!

4'

this one allowed grazing

Cutter          Stirrer

ox-cart ruggle

a Silage Chopper

a Winnower

a Ruggle or Drag-Shoe

to keep a heavily laden wagon from rolling over the horses downhill.

3½ ft.

c. 1850

a Washing Stick (before scrubbing-boards)

a Lard Squeezer

hide hinge

Eel spears

# Index

Adze
    carpenter's, 27
    cooper's, 29
    gutter, 27
    hand, 29
    Indian, 29
    shipwright's, 27
Anvil
    beak, 91
    colonial, 90
    nailer's, 93
    oliver, 93
    stake, 90
Apple
    barrow, 47
    butter paddles, 47
    butter stirrers, 47
    quarterer, 34
Auger
    burn, 73
    fruit, 83
    nose, 73
    pod, 73
    ream, 73
    spoon, 73
    spiral, 72
    tap, 75
    taper, 74
    twisted, 73
Awl
    burning, 73
    ream, 73
Axe
    Anglo-American, 11
    brick, 99
    British, 11, 13
    chisel, 12
    German, 11, 13
    ice, 99
    joiner's, 13
    Kent, 13
    mortise, 12
    shipbuilder's, 13

    trade, 12
    triangular, 11
    Yankee, 51

Bark
    axe, 49
    chisel, 49
    irons, 49
    mill, 48
    spuds, 49
Beak iron, 91
Bec d'ane, 50
Beetle, 30
Bench clamp, 9
Bit
    center, 77
    gouge, 73
    nose, 73
    spoon, 73
    twist, 73
Blacksmith tools, 90, 91
Block knife, 9, 85
Bog cutter, 85
Bore
    hooked reamer, 75
    taper, 74
    wheelwright's reamer, 75
Boring machine, 77
Box vise, 9
Brace
    coachmaker's, 78
    natural shape, 79
    pumpkin-handled, 81
Broad axe
    American, 15
    goose-wing, 15
    how used, 16, 17
    polless, 15
    straight-handled, 18
Bull rake, 102
Bungstart, 23
Butteris, 91

*About the Author*

ERIC SLOANE has written many books about Early American times and has collected for research purposes the tools, sometimes ingeniously devised, often exquisitely constructed, that our crafts-respecting forefathers made, with which they carved those delightful pieces and useful articles that made up the wonderful hand-made world of yesterday.

No worshiper of old things for the sake of age alone, Sloane collects only the good things of the past and tries to reintroduce the Early American philosophy of excellence to the present generation. Why would a backwoods farmer forge an axe with classic decorations on it? Where did the maker of this hand-made tool get his knowledge of Greek symmetry? Mr. Sloane enjoys describing those accomplishments of a proud and individualistic world, in the hope that the reader will remember something worthwhile that otherwise would be forgotten in this present world of rapid changes and mass production.